ANDREW WHITE

Don't be like Max! Simple Steps To A Debt Free Life.

First edition

This book was professionally typeset on Reedsy.
Find out more at reedsy.com

Contents

1

Introduction

In a world where financial stability is coveted, many individuals struggle to keep their spending habits in check. Meet Max, an average person working full time, striving to make ends meet. Despite having a steady income, Max finds himself continuously tempted to spend money he doesn't have. Whether it's the allure of financing a new truck, going on vacations on credit card, or impulsive shopping sprees to buy things he wants but doesn't need.

Max often finds himself spending more money than he earns.

Max's story is common. Many people face similar challenges when it comes to managing their finances effectively. It's all too easy to fall into the trap of overspending, accumulating debt, and struggling to make ends meet.

Don't be like Max!

The tremendous power of controlling your money lies at the

core of your financial transformation. It's time to stop letting money control you and empower yourself with knowledge and skills to shape and direct your financial future.

2

Facing the Reality of Debt

Acknowledging the Problem

Dealing with debt can be overwhelming, but facing the reality of your situation head-on is crucial if you want to change your financial circumstances. This section will help you acknowledge the problem and understand why it's important to take action.

When it comes to debt, it's easy to stick our heads in the sand and avoid confronting the issue. However, avoiding the problem only prolongs the cycle of debt and prevents us from moving towards financial freedom.

But here's the thing - acknowledging the problem is the first step towards finding a solution. By recognizing debt's impact on our lives and understanding the consequences of inaction, we can gather the motivation and determination to overcome it.

Think about it. How does it feel to live with the constant weight of debt on your shoulders? Does money stress keep you up at night? Do you feel trapped and limited in your choices? Acknowledging these emotional impacts can help fuel your desire for change.

I know firsthand how daunting it can be to face the reality of being in debt. I've been there. But I also know that there is a way out, and it starts with acknowledging the problem and committing to take control of your financial future.

So, take a moment to reflect on your current debt situation. Be honest with yourself about the challenges it presents and how it's affecting your life. Recognize the emotional toll it's taking on you and use that as fuel to propel yourself forward.

Remember, you're not alone in this journey. Countless others have faced similar struggles and come out on top. By acknowledging the problem, you're already one step closer to finding the solutions to turn your financial situation around. You can take control and create a brighter future for yourself.

Understanding the Impact of Debt

As someone who has experienced the burden of debt firsthand, I understand how it can negatively impact your financial well-being. But don't worry, there is hope! This sub chapter will delve into how debt can significantly affect your life and provide you with the motivation and tools to turn your situation around.

Debt affects your bank account and seeps into various aspects of your personal and professional life. Let's take a closer look at the impact it can have:

1. **Financial Stress:** Debt can be extremely stressful. It hangs over your head like a dark cloud, causing sleepless nights and constant worry. The constant pressure to meet monthly payments can create an endless cycle of stress, affecting your overall well-being and mental health.

2. **Limited Financial Freedom:** When you're in debt, a significant portion of your income goes towards repaying it. This means you have less money to spend on things you enjoy, such as vacations, hobbies, and even daily pleasures. Debt restricts your financial freedom and can make you feel trapped.

3. **Damaged Credit Score:** Debt can wreak havoc on your credit score. Late payments, defaults, or high credit utilization can negatively impact your creditworthiness. A poor credit score can make securing new credit, renting a home, or even getting a job difficult.

4. **Strained Relationships:** Financial stress caused by debt can strain relationships with your loved ones. It can lead to arguments, resentment, and even a communication breakdown. Debt can strain your relationships tremendously, making it crucial to address and resolve it.

5. **Reduced Career Opportunities:** Debt can also significantly impact your professional life. It hinders your ability to take risks, pursue new career opportunities, or make bold moves. The fear of financial instability may make you less inclined to follow your dreams or take on meaningful professional challenges.

Now that we've explored how debt can negatively impact your life, don't lose hope! In the following sections, we will look deeper into understanding the long-term effects of debt on your personal and professional life. I will share practical tips, strategies, and motivation to help you overcome debt and regain control over your financial future.

3

Assessing Your Financial Situation

Calculating Total Debt

Learning to calculate your total debt accurately is an essential step towards improving your financial situation and taking control of your debts. It's not just about knowing how much you owe but also understanding the different types of loans and their impact on your overall debt. Let's dive into the world of debt calculations and get a clear picture of where you stand.

Calculating your total debt involves considering all types of loans, such as credit card debt, personal loans, mortgages, and personal loans. Start by gathering all the necessary information, including each loan's current balances, interest rates, and monthly payment obligations.

Once you have gathered all the required information, it's time to crunch the numbers. Add up the outstanding balances of all your loans, including any interest or fees that have accrued. This will give you the total amount you currently owe. Remember that the interest rates can be variable or fixed, so include both.

Now, let's take a closer look at the importance of tracking down every outstanding debt you have. It's crucial to thoroughly understand your debts to effectively manage them and work towards becoming debt-free. Listing down all your outstanding debts will allow you to prioritize your repayment strategy and identify potential areas where you can save money.

Start by making a comprehensive list of all your debts, including credit card balances, personal loans, and any other outstanding liabilities that you may have. Include the unpaid balance, interest rate, minimum monthly payment, and the total amount owed.

Tracking down every debt will help you gain a clear understanding of your overall financial situation. It can be an eye-opening experience and might even motivate you to take immediate action. Remember, getting out of debt is not an overnight process, but with patience and a well-planned approach, you can make steady progress toward financial freedom.

Understanding Interest Rates

Interest rates can significantly impact the overall cost of debt, and understanding them is crucial if you want to improve your financial situation. In this sub chapter, we will delve into the world of interest rates, exploring their various types and how they can affect your debt. So, let's dive in and unlock the secrets of interest rates!

Interest rates can be quite complex to comprehend, but fear not! I will guide you through the intricacies and help you understand it all. Sit down, get a cup of coffee, and prepare to become an interest rate aficionado.

Let's start with the basics - the simple interest rate. This type of interest is calculated on the principal amount of your debt. It doesn't consider any additional charges, fees, or compounding. That means that the interest stays the same throughout the life of your loan, making it much easier to calculate and predict.

Depending on your financial goals, a simple interest rate can be an advantage or a disadvantage. A simple interest rate might be ideal for you if you are looking for stability and predictability. However, you should explore other options to save on interest payments.

Now, let's move on to the compound interest rate. This type of interest is a bit more complex but can significantly impact your debt. Unlike simple interest, compound interest considers not only the principal amount but also the accumulated interest charges. These charges are added to the initial amount, and the interest is then calculated on the new total. If left unchecked, this compounding effect will lead to exponential growth in your debt.

Understanding compound interest is essential for anyone look-ing to manage their debt effectively. Knowing how it works, you can devise strategies to minimize the impact and save thousands of dollars in interest payments.

Another type of interest rate you may encounter is the fixed interest rate. As the name suggests, this rate remains constant throughout the life of your loan. It offers stability and predictability, allowing you to budget your payments without worrying about fluctuations in interest rates.

Fixed interest rates can be an excellent choice if you prefer long-term planning and want to avoid any surprises. However, they may not be the most advantageous option if interest rates drop significantly during the life of your loan, as you won't benefit from the lower rates.

On the flip side, we have a variable interest rate. This rate type is not set in stone but fluctuates based on external factors such as economic conditions and market trends. While variable interest rates can initially be lower than fixed rates, they can also rise significantly over time.

Variable interest rates are a choice for those who are comfortable with uncertainty and willing to take on some risk. If you believe that interest rates will remain low or are confident in your ability to handle higher payments, a variable rate might be the way to go.

Understanding interest rates is crucial for anyone with debt or seeking financial improvement. Whether it's the simplicity of a fixed rate or the potential savings from a variable rate, each type has its own advantages and drawbacks. By arming yourself with knowledge, you can make informed decisions about your financial situation and take control of your debt.

Creating a Budget

Imagine the peace of mind that comes with managing your debt effectively. No more sleepless nights, no more constant worry about bills piling up. Creating a budget can be the first step towards financial freedom and regaining control over your finances. It's time to explore the significance of creating a budget for managing debt effectively.

A budget serves as your road map to financial stability. It helps you understand where your money is going and allows you to make informed decisions about your spending. By tracking your income and expenses, you can identify areas where you can cut back and allocate more funds towards debt repayment.

Moreover, creating a budget empowers you to take control of your debt. It gives you a clear picture of how much you owe and helps you prioritize your debt repayment strategy. With a budget in place, you can make a plan to pay off your debts systematically and avoid falling into further financial trouble.

Now that you understand the importance of creating a budget let's delve into the art of allocating funds toward debt repayment in a balanced way.

Effective debt management starts with assessing your income and expenses. Determine how much money you have available each month after covering your essential expenses like rent, utilities, and groceries. This will be the amount you can allocate towards debt repayment.

It's crucial to strike a balance between debt repayment and maintaining a reasonable standard of living. While throwing all your extra money towards debt may be tempting, ensuring that you have enough left over for emergencies and unexpected expenses is essential. And remember, it's okay to treat yourself occasionally as long as it fits within your budget.

As you allocate funds towards debt repayment, prioritize high-interest debts, such as credit cards or personal loans, to save on interest charges in the long run. Use the snowball or avalanche method to pay off your debts systematically and stay motivated throughout the journey.

Remember, managing debt is not an overnight process. It requires discipline, determination, and a well-planned budget. So, let's roll up our sleeves, create a budget, and take the first step towards financial freedom and a debt-free future.

Creating a budget is the key to managing your debt effectively. It enables you to take control of your finances and make conscious decisions about your spending and debt repayment. Let me guide you through the process of creating a budget that works for you:

1. Start by tracking your income: List down all sources of income, including your salary, freelance work, or any additional sources of income. This will give you a clear idea of how much money you have coming in each month.
2. Next, track your expenses: Write down all your expenses, including fixed costs like rent or mortgage payments, car

payments, utility bills, Phone bills and groceries, as well as variable expenses like dining out, entertainment, and shopping. It's essential to be thorough and include every expense, no matter how small.

3. Analyze your spending: Once you have a complete list of your income and expenses, it's time to analyze your spending patterns. Identify areas where you can cut back and save money. You can reduce your dining-out expenses or find a more affordable phone plan. Every dollar saved can be allocated towards debt repayment.

4. Set financial goals: Determine how much money you want to allocate towards monthly debt repayment. Set realistic goals that are attainable within your budget. A clear target will keep you motivated and focused on your debt repayment journey.

5. Create a debt repayment plan: Prioritize your debts based on interest rates and outstanding balances. Consider using the snowball or avalanche method to pay off your debts systematically. The snowball method involves paying off the smallest debt first, while the avalanche method focuses on paying off debts with the highest interest rates first.

6. Please stick to your budget: Once you have created a budget and a debt repayment plan, it's crucial to stick to it. Avoid unnecessary expenses, stay disciplined, and remember your financial goals. Remember, every dollar allocated towards debt repayment brings you one step closer to financial freedom.

Creating a budget is the first step towards managing your debt effectively. It provides structure, clarity, and control over your finances. By following these steps and committing to your budget, you'll be on your way to a debt-free future.

4

Changing Your Mindset

Shifting Your Perspective on Money

Changing your mindset towards money is a vital step toward debt freedom. It's not just about finding ways to pay off your debts; it's about transforming your relationship with money so that you can live a financially secure and fulfilling life. This shift in perspective is essential for long-term success, and it all starts with recognizing the importance of changing your mindset.

You quickly feel overwhelmed, stressed, and even defeated when you have debt. But by changing your mindset, you can regain control and start making positive changes. Instead of seeing debt as a burden, you can see it as an opportunity for growth and personal development. This shift in perspective allows you to approach your financial situation with a sense of empowerment and determination.

Recognizing the impact of your financial habits and beliefs is a significant step towards staying debt-free. Your habits and beliefs play a crucial role in shaping your financial future. It's important to understand that debt is not just a result of external factors; it is often the consequence of our actions and choices.

To break free from debt and stay debt-free, developing healthier financial habits is essential. This means being mindful of your spending, creating a budget, and finding ways to save money. It also means changing your beliefs about money and adopting a more positive and abundant mindset. Instead of viewing money as a scarce resource, start seeing it as a tool to help you achieve your goals and live your desired life.

Shifting your perspective on money is not always easy, but it is essential for your financial well-being. It requires determination, discipline, and a commitment to change. But the rewards are well worth the effort. By changing your mindset and developing healthier financial habits, you can break free from debt and create a brighter financial future for yourself.

5

Developing a Repayment Plan

Setting Realistic Goals

When tackling your debt, setting achievable goals is critical to success. It's essential to understand the significance of setting realistic milestones that will help you stay motivated and on track toward becoming debt-free. This subchapter will explore the importance of setting achievable goals and how to break down your debt into smaller milestones.

Setting Realistic Goals:

Setting realistic goals is one of the most crucial aspects of achieving financial freedom. It's easy to feel overwhelmed by the amount of debt you have accumulated but remember that Rome wasn't built in a day. Breaking down your debt repayment journey into smaller, achievable goals will make the process less daunting and provide you with a sense of accomplishment as you reach each milestone.

When setting your goals, it's essential to consider your current financial situation, income, and expenses. Consider what is feasible for you to achieve within a specific time frame. Setting unrealistic goals may lead to frustration and discouragement, ultimately derailing your progress. Be honest with yourself and set goals that are challenging yet attainable.

Stay Motivated:

As you embark on your debt repayment journey, staying motivated throughout the process is vital. Setting realistic goals effectively keeps you motivated and focused on your ultimate objective of becoming debt-free. By breaking down your debt into smaller milestones, you'll be able to monitor your progress and see the impact of your efforts.

Remember, motivation can come from various sources. Consider using visual aids such as a progress chart or a vision board to track your achievements and remind yourself of the financial freedom you are working towards. Additionally, surround yourself with a supportive community of friends or family members who can provide encouragement and accountability along the way.

Celebrate Your Success:

Each time you achieve one of your smaller milestones, it's essential to celebrate your success. Recognize and reward yourself for the progress you have made. Celebrating these victories, no matter how small they may seem, will help to reinforce your commitment and motivate you to keep going.

Whether treating yourself to a small indulgence, planning a self-care day, or simply acknowledging your achievement, find a way to mark the occasion. Celebrating your success provides a sense of accomplishment and a reminder of how far you have come on your debt repayment journey.

Exploring Debt Repayment Strategies

When tackling debt, it's essential to have a solid repayment strategy in place. This sub chapter will explore different debt repayment strategies that can help you make significant progress in paying off your debts. Let's dive in!

One popular strategy is the snowball method. This approach involves prioritizing your debts based on their balance, from smallest to largest. Start by making minimum payments on all your debts, then focus on paying off the smallest one first. Once that debt is paid off, add the amount you were paying towards it to the minimum payment of the next smallest debt. This process creates a snowball effect, where the momentum of paying off one debt motivates you to tackle the next one. Not only does this method help to eliminate debts quicker, but it also provides a sense of accomplishment along the way.

Another strategy to consider is the avalanche method. This method prioritizes debts based on their interest rates, starting with the highest interest rate first. Focusing on high-interest debts can save money on interest payments in the long run. Like the snowball method, you continue to make minimum payments on all your debts but put any extra funds towards the debt with the highest interest rate. Once that debt is paid off, you move on to the next highest interest-rate debt. The avalanche method may take longer to see tangible results than the snowball method, but it can save you more money overall.

Now that you have an overview of these two popular debt repayment strategies, it's time to reflect on your specific circumstances and goals. Consider your financial situation and personal preferences to determine which strategy resonates most. Remember, the key to successfully paying off debt is consistency and perseverance. It's essential to stay motivated throughout the process.

Additionally, it's crucial to understand when to prioritize high-interest debts or debts with lower balances. While both strategies have their merits, analyzing your situation carefully is essential. If you have debts with high-interest rates, prioritize them first to reduce the overall cost of borrowing. However, if you have debts with smaller balances, you may find it more motivating to start with those first to eliminate them quickly.

6

Generating Additional Income

Exploring Side Hustles

Are you drowning in financial debt and searching for ways to turn your situation around? Well, you're in luck! This sub chapter will explore various side hustle opportunities that can help you generate extra income and improve your financial standing.

Now, let's dive in and discover some fantastic side hustles that can significantly impact your finances!

1. **Freelancing:** If you have a skill or expertise in a particular field, why not consider freelancing? You can offer your services as a freelance writer, graphic designer, web developer, or any other skill you possess. Platforms like Upwork and Freelancer can connect you with potential clients and help you kickstart your freelancing career.
2. **Renting out your space**: Do you have a spare room or an

unused apartment? Consider utilizing it as a source of income by listing it on platforms like Airbnb. You can earn extra cash by renting your space to travelers or short-term visitors.

3. **Starting a blog or YouTube channel**: If you are passionate about writing or creating content, starting a blog or YouTube channel can be a rewarding side hustle. By monetizing your blog through ads or partnering with brands on YouTube, you can generate income based on your audience and viewership numbers.

4. **Driving for ride-sharing services**: If you own a car and enjoy driving, signing up for rides like Uber or Lyft can be a flexible way to earn extra income. You can choose your hours and work whenever it suits your schedule.

5. **Becoming a virtual assistant**: Many businesses and entrepreneurs require virtual assistants to help with email management, social media scheduling, and data entry tasks. Becoming a virtual assistant can be a lucrative side hustle if you have strong organizational and communication skills.

By exploring these side hustle opportunities, you can leverage your existing skills and hobbies to generate additional income and improve your financial situation. Remember, consistency and dedication are crucial to succeeding in any side hustle. So, don't be afraid to put in the extra effort and take your financial journey into your own hands!

7

Managing Debt Collection Calls

Dealing with Debt Collectors

Are you tired of the constant stress and worry that comes with being in debt?

Do debt collection calls make you feel overwhelmed and anxious? Well, you're not alone. Many people struggle to manage their finances in a similar situation.

But don't worry because this subchapter will delve into the world of debt collectors and provide practical strategies to handle their calls professionally. By the end of this section, you'll feel empowered and equipped to take control of your financial situation.

Now, let's dive right in!

First and foremost, it's essential to understand your consumer rights and the protections afforded to you when dealing with debt collectors. These rights exist to ensure fair treatment and prevent harassment or abusive behavior.

But how exactly do you protect yourself? Well, that's where knowledge is power! By familiarizing yourself with these rights and regulations, you'll know exactly what a debt collector can and cannot do.

For instance, did you know that debt collectors are not allowed to call you at unreasonable hours, such as early in the morning or late at night? They also cannot harass, threaten, or use any abusive language while trying to collect a debt.

Furthermore, debt collectors must provide you with information about the debt they are trying to collect. This includes the original creditor's name, the amount owed, and an explanation of your rights as a consumer.

By being aware of your rights, you can confidently assert yourself in dealing with debt collectors. Remember, you have the right to be treated with respect and dignity throughout the process.

Now that you have a solid foundation of your rights let's move on to the strategies that will help you handle debt collection calls like a pro.

Firstly, it's crucial to stay calm and composed during these calls. Remember, the person on the other end of the line is just doing their job. Maintaining a professional and courteous tone can create a more productive conversation.

Secondly, always verify the accuracy of the debt being claimed. Debt collectors may sometimes pursue debts that are not yours or are past the statute of limitations. Take the time to gather all relevant information and ask for documented proof of the debt.

Lastly, if you cannot pay the debt immediately, consider negotiating a repayment plan that works within your budget. Debt collectors are often willing to cooperate if they believe a realistic plan is being made.

Remember, tackling your debt won't happen overnight. It takes time, patience, and a strong mindset. But by applying the strategies discussed in this subchapter, you're already on your way to improving your financial situation.

Negotiating Repayment Plans

I know that dealing with financial debt can feel overwhelming, but there are negotiation techniques that can help you create manageable repayment plans with your creditors. By taking a proactive approach and effectively communicating with your creditors, you can work towards improving your financial situation.

When negotiating repayment plans with your creditors, gathering all the necessary information about your debts is essential. This includes the total amount owed, interest rates, and applicable fees or penalties. A clear understanding of your financial situation will empower you during the negotiation process.

Once you have gathered all the relevant information, it's time to start negotiating. Remember, the key to successful negotiation is being prepared and confident. Approach your creditors positively, and express your willingness to work out a mutually beneficial solution.

Start by explaining your current financial struggles and why you cannot make full payments. Being honest and transparent about your situation will help build trust with your creditors. Show them you are committed to resolving your debts and actively seeking solutions.

Offer a repayment plan that is feasible for you based on your current financial circumstances. This may involve proposing reduced monthly payments or extended repayment terms. Be realistic about what you can afford, and be prepared to provide evidence of your income and expenses to support your proposed plan.

During the negotiation process, listening to your creditors and considering their considerations is crucial. They may have suggestions or alternative options that work better for both parties. Be open to these suggestions and be willing to make compromises if necessary.

Throughout the negotiation process, maintain proactive communication with your creditors. Regularly update them on your progress and provide documentation to support your repayment plan. This could include bank statements, pay stubs, or other relevant financial information. Keeping your creditors informed and involved will help build trust and cooperation.

Remember, negotiations can sometimes be challenging and may require persistence. Keep going even if initial proposals are rejected. Stay positive, keep exploring different options, and maintain open lines of communication. Your creditors will notice your commitment and effort; together, you can work towards finding a manageable repayment plan.

By utilizing these negotiation techniques, you can take control of your financial debt and pave the way toward a more secure financial future. Remember, the key is to be proactive, communicate effectively, and be willing to find mutually beneficial solutions. Don't let debt define you – take charge and create a plan for a brighter tomorrow.

8

Exploring Debt Consolidation Options

Understanding the Pros and Cons

Let's dive into debt consolidation and explore its pros and cons. If you're dealing with financial debt and want to change your situation, this sub chapter is tailored just for you. We'll examine the advantages and disadvantages of debt consolidation as a debt management option. So, let's get started and empower ourselves with the knowledge we need to make an informed decision.

Debt consolidation has several advantages that can help individuals tackle their financial burdens more effectively. These benefits may include:

- 1. **Streamlined Payments**: Debt consolidation allows you to combine multiple debts into a monthly payment. This helps simplify your financial life by eliminating the need to keep track of multiple payment deadlines and amounts.
- 2. **Lower Interest Rates**: By consolidating your debts, you

may secure a lower interest rate. In the long run, this can save you money, as you'll pay less interest over time.

- 3. **Improved Organization**: With debt consolidation, you'll have a clearer picture of your overall debt situation. This can help you better understand the scope of your financial obligations and develop a more effective repayment plan.
- 4. **Potential for Debt Reduction**: Some debt consolidation programs or loans offer the possibility of reducing your overall debt amount. Negotiating lower payoff amounts or settling outstanding balances can help you get closer to debt freedom.
- 5. **Mental Relief**: Dealing with multiple debts can be overwhelming and stressful. Debt consolidation can provide mental relief by simplifying your debt management and giving you control over your financial situation.

While debt consolidation offers several advantages, it's also essential to consider the potential downsides. Here are some cons to keep in mind:

- 1. **Extended Repayment Period**: Consolidating your debts may result in a more extended repayment period. While this can lead to smaller monthly payments, you may pay more in total interest over time.
- 2. **Potential for Higher Costs**: Depending on the terms of your consolidation option, additional fees or costs may be involved. It's crucial to thoroughly understand the fees associated with the consolidation process before deciding.
- 3. **Requirement for Collateral**: Some debt consolidation options, such as secured loans, may require collateral, such as your home or car. This can put your assets at risk if you

cannot make the consolidated loan payments.

- 4. **Temporarily Impact on Credit Score**: The debt consolidation process can initially negatively impact your credit score. However, your credit score can gradually improve if you make consistent payments on time.
- 5. **Potential for Continued Spending Habits**: Debt consolidation clears your existing debts but doesn't address the underlying causes of financial trouble. Without managing spending habits and budgeting, there's a risk of falling back into debt after consolidating.

Remember, before opting for debt consolidation, examining your specific financial circumstances and consulting with a financial advisor is crucial. Analyze the advantages and disadvantages to ensure it aligns with your goals and helps you take control of your financial future. With the right approach and commitment, debt consolidation can be a powerful tool in your journey towards financial freedom.

Researching Different Consolidation Methods

When it comes to managing debt, exploring various debt consolidation methods can be a significant step toward improving your financial situation. In this subchapter, we will dive into the process of researching different consolidation methods and provide you with the necessary tools to make an informed decision.

One common method of debt consolidation is through balance transfers. This involves transferring the balances from high-interest rate credit cards to a new credit card with a lower interest rate. Doing so can save money on interest payments and simplify your debt by combining multiple payments into one.

Another viable option is taking out a personal loan for debt consolidation. This allows you to borrow a lump sum to pay off your debts, and then you can focus on repaying the loan gradually over time. Personal loans often have lower interest rates than credit cards, making them an attractive choice for many individuals seeking to consolidate their debt.

When researching different consolidation methods, it is crucial to consider certain factors. Firstly, compare the interest rates lenders or credit card companies offer to ensure you get a favorable rate. Additionally, consider the repayment terms and any associated fees or charges. Choosing a consolidation method that aligns with your budget and financial goals is essential.

Furthermore, take the time to read reviews or seek recommendations from trusted sources. This can provide insights into the experiences of others who have used a particular consolidation method and help you weigh the pros and cons. Additionally, consider consulting with a financial advisor or credit counselor who can provide valuable guidance and assistance.

Lastly, when evaluating your options for debt consolidation, be sure to take into account any potential impact on your credit score. While consolidation can positively affect your credit by simplifying your debt and improving your payment history, it is essential to plan your payments and avoid any missed or late fees, as this can hurt your credit score.

By researching and evaluating different consolidation methods, you can take control of your debt and work towards a brighter financial future. Remember, each individual's financial situation is unique, so choosing a consolidation method that suits your specific needs and goals is crucial. With determination and commitment, you can overcome debt and enjoy peace of mind with a healthier financial outlook.

9

Building and Repairing Credit

Understanding Credit Scores

When managing your debt and overall financial health, one crucial aspect that cannot be ignored is your credit score. Your credit score holds significant importance as it determines your creditworthiness and impacts your ability to secure loans or favorable interest rates. This sub chapter will delve deep into the world of credit scores, understanding their significance, and empowering you with knowledge to improve them.

Understanding credit scores is the first step towards taking control of your financial situation. Your credit score is a numerical representation of your creditworthiness based on your credit history and financial behavior. This three-digit number can range from 300 to 850, with a higher score indicating better creditworthiness. The score is calculated by credit bureaus using complex algorithms, taking into account various factors.

The factors that affect your credit score include payment history, credit utilization, length of credit history, types of credit used, and new credit inquiries. Each factor carries different weights, and comprehending their impact is crucial in improving your credit score. Maintaining a history of timely payments, keeping your credit utilization low, and having a diverse credit mix can positively influence your credit score.

It is also essential to understand that your credit score is not fixed and can be improved over time through conscious efforts. Developing responsible financial habits and making strategic choices can boost your credit score and pave the way toward a better financial future. The following sections will explore effective strategies to enhance your credit score, providing a roadmap to success.

Improving Credit History

Rebuilding and improving your credit history after debt repayment can seem daunting, but with the right strategies and mindset, it is possible to achieve. In this subchapter, I will provide some practical steps and tips to help you improve your credit history and set yourself up for a debt-free life.

First and foremost, it is essential to understand the significance of having a good credit history. Your credit history is a reflection of your financial behavior, and it plays a crucial role in determining your future creditworthiness. Lenders, landlords, and even potential employers may review your credit history to assess how responsible you are for managing money. Therefore, taking proactive steps to improve your credit history is essential.

To begin rebuilding your credit history, the first step is to obtain a copy of your credit report. This report will provide insights into your current credit standing, including any outstanding debts, late payments, or defaults. Carefully review your credit report to identify errors or discrepancies, as these can negatively impact your credit score. If you spot any inaccuracies, make sure to report them to the credit bureaus and take the necessary steps to rectify them.

Next, developing a realistic budget and sticking to it religiously is crucial. A budget will help you keep track of your income and expenses, ensuring that you are living within your means and meeting your financial obligations. By carefully managing your finances, you can minimize the risk of falling into debt again and demonstrate responsible credit behavior.

When it comes to credit, it is essential to use it wisely. While it may be tempting to avoid credit altogether, having a positive credit history is crucial for future financial endeavors. Start by obtaining a secured credit card or a small personal loan that you can easily manage. Making timely payments on these accounts will demonstrate your financial responsibility and gradually rebuild your credit history.

Another effective strategy to improve your credit history is to become an authorized user on someone else's credit card. Choose someone with a good credit history and responsible credit behavior. By being associated with their account, you can benefit from their positive credit history and improve your credit score.

Lastly, be patient and persistent. Rebuilding and improving your credit history takes time and effort. Staying committed to your financial goals and making responsible credit choices consistently is essential. Keep a close eye on your credit score and monitor your progress. As you see improvements in your credit history, your motivation will soar, and you will be one step closer to a debt-free life.

Improving your credit history requires financial discipline, responsible credit management, and patience. Following the strategies outlined in this sub chapter and staying committed to your financial goals, you can rebuild and improve your credit history, setting the foundation for a brighter financial future.

10

Staying Committed to a Debt-Free Life

Overcoming Temptations

This sub chapter will dive deep into overcoming temptations and equip you with practical tips to improve your financial situation.

One of the key factors in overcoming temptations is self-awareness. Understanding why you're prone to impulsive spending and what triggers those tendencies is essential. You'll be better equipped to resist temptation by identifying patterns and recognizing your triggers.

Let's start by acknowledging that overcoming temptations is not an easy journey. It requires determination, willpower, and a strong mindset. However, always remember that you have the power to take control of your financial situation and build a better future.

The first step is to create a realistic budget and stick to it. It's crucial to track your expenses and prioritize your needs over wants.

Setting clear financial goals and monitoring your progress will make you less likely to give in to impulsive purchases.

Another helpful technique is implementing a waiting period before making significant purchases. When you feel the urge to buy something impulsively, give yourself time to think it over. Often, you'll find that the desire fades away, and you can make a more rational decision.

Sometimes, surrounding yourself with supportive people can make a world of difference. Seek a partner, friend, or family member to hold you accountable for your spending habits. This person can help you stay on track and remind you of your goals when temptations arise.

Additionally, find alternative ways to engage in activities that bring you joy without breaking your budget. Explore free or low-cost hobbies, such as reading, walking, or volunteering. Focusing on experiences rather than material possessions will make you less likely to succumb to impulsive spending.

Lastly, don't be too hard on yourself if you slip up occasionally. Overcoming temptations takes time, and setbacks are a natural part of the process. Learn from your mistakes, analyze what led to the lapse, and use it as an opportunity to grow stronger and more resilient.

Remember, you are capable of achieving financial stability and overcoming temptations. Stay focused, stay motivated, and stay committed to your goal. With the right strategies and a positive mindset, you can break free from debt and create a brighter future for yourself!

Seeking Support from Family and Friends

Now that you have decided to embark on a journey towards becoming debt-free, it's essential to surround yourself with a support system that will keep you motivated and accountable. One of the most powerful sources of support comes from your family and friends. They can provide the encouragement and motivation you need to stay committed to your goal. In this subchapter, we will explore how you can seek support from your loved ones.

1. **Communicate your goals:**

It's crucial to have open and honest communication with your family and friends about your financial situation and your goal of becoming debt-free. By sharing your goals, you are creating accountability and allowing them to understand and support your journey. Discussing your plans will also help them realize the importance of their support in your success.

2. **Seek emotional support:**

Dealing with debt can be stressful and emotionally draining. That's where your loved ones come in. Share your concerns, fears, and challenges with them. Let them be there for you to provide emotional support and reassurance during difficult times. Having someone who understands what you're going through can make a difference.

3. Share progress updates:

Regularly updating your family and friends about your progress can help you stay motivated and accountable. Whether it's paying off a significant portion of your debt or making a financial decision that aligns with your goals, sharing these milestones can inspire others and serve as a way to celebrate your achievements together.

4. Involve them in your journey:

Your loved ones can play an active role in supporting your debt-free journey. Encourage your family and friends to join you in making conscious financial decisions, such as budgeting, saving money, and finding affordable alternatives for leisure activities. By involving them in your journey, you create a sense of camaraderie and shared commitment towards a debt-free life.

5. Ask for accountability:

Sometimes, we all need a little push to stay on track. Don't hesitate to ask your family and friends to hold you accountable for your financial decisions. Whether reminding you to stick to your budget, questioning unnecessary purchases, or gently challenging your spending habits, their accountability can keep you focused and motivated.

Remember, the road to debt-free can be challenging, but having the support of your loved ones can make it easier and more rewarding. By communicating your goals, seeking emotional support, sharing progress updates, involving them in your journey, and asking for accountability, you can leverage the power of social support and stay committed to your debt-free life.

11

Celebrating Financial Milestones

When it comes to achieving debt freedom, one of the most crucial steps is to track and measure your progress along the way. It's essential to clearly understand where you currently stand financially and how far you've come since you started your journey towards debt repayment. This sub chapter will explore various methods you can use to track your progress effectively.

In today's digital age, numerous financial apps and tools can help you monitor and track your financial progress. These apps enable you to record your income, expenses, and debt payments, providing real-time updates on your financial health. By utilizing these tools, you can easily visualize your progress and gain insights into areas where you can improve.

Sometimes, seeing your progress visually can be incredibly motivating. Consider creating a visual progress board or chart to track your debt repayment journey. Whether it's a simple poster, a spreadsheet with color-coded cells, or a digital chart on your computer, find a method that resonates with you. Update it regularly as you make payments, and watch your progress unfold before your eyes. This tangible representation of your journey can provide a powerful boost of motivation.

Tracking your progress becomes much more meaningful when you have specific financial goals. Set clear targets for yourself, such as paying off a certain amount of debt within a particular timeframe or reaching a specific debt-to-income ratio. Break down these goals into smaller, achievable milestones. As you accomplish each milestone, record your progress and celebrate your success. This way, you'll have a concrete way to measure your advancement and keep yourself motivated throughout your debt repayment journey.

Another method to track your financial progress is by regularly reviewing your bank, credit card, and loan statements. Take the time to analyze your income and expenses, identifying areas where you can cut back or improve. By staying on top of your financial statements, you can understand your cash flow and make informed decisions that will accelerate your progress toward debt freedom.

Tracking progress isn't just about the numbers; it's also about recognizing the emotional journey you're undertaking. Consider keeping a journal to document your thoughts, feelings, and achievements. Journaling allows you to reflect on your progress, acknowledge the challenges you've overcome, and celebrate the milestones you've achieved. It can be a powerful reminder of your resilience and dedication in facing financial adversity.

Remember, tracking your progress is not just about keeping a record; it's about staying engaged and motivated throughout your journey toward debt freedom. Explore the methods mentioned here and find the ones that resonate most with you. By actively tracking and measuring your progress, you'll be empowered to make better financial decisions and ultimately achieve your dream of debt-free life.

Rewarding Yourself for Achievements

One of the most important aspects of getting out of debt is rewarding yourself for achieving milestones. Acknowledging and celebrating your progress to stay motivated and continue on your path to financial freedom is crucial. This section will delve into various affordable and meaningful ways to reward yourself for debt-free achievements.

When it comes to rewarding yourself, finding activities or treats that align with your financial goal is essential. You don't want to undo all the hard work you've put into paying off your debts by overspending or indulging in unnecessary luxuries. Instead, focus on activities that provide a sense of joy and accomplishment without breaking the bank.

One meaningful way to reward yourself for achieving debt-free milestones is by engaging in experiences that enhance your overall well-being. For example, you could treat yourself to a relaxing spa day or a weekend getaway in nature. These experiences offer a chance to rejuvenate and recharge while celebrating your progress.

Another affordable way to reward yourself is by indulging in hobbies or interests that bring you happiness. Whether it's painting, playing an instrument, or even gardening, these activities provide a source of enjoyment and remind you of the progress you've made in taking control of your financial situation.

Physical rewards can also be a great way to celebrate your debt-free achievements. Consider purchasing something on your wishlist for a while, such as a new book, a piece of clothing, or a gadget. Remember to set a reasonable budget for these rewards and stick to it. The idea is to treat yourself without compromising your newfound financial freedom.

Lastly, pay attention to the power of small, meaningful gestures. Sometimes, a simple handwritten note to yourself, acknowledging your accomplishments and expressing gratitude for the journey, can be just as rewarding as any material indulgence. These acts of self-appreciation remind you how far you've come and can help solidify your commitment to staying debt-free.

Remember, rewarding yourself is an important part of the debt-free journey. By celebrating your milestones in affordable and meaningful ways, you'll stay motivated and continue to make progress toward financial freedom.

12

Conclusion

Staying motivated on your debt-free journey goes beyond superficial strategies.

It requires a deeper understanding of setting clear goals, tracking progress, celebrating milestones, seeking support, visualizing your future, practicing self-care, learning from setbacks, staying educated, and aligning with your "why.

" By implementing these strategies, you can maintain motivation, overcome obstacles, and successfully achieve your debt-free goal. Embrace the journey, stay resolute, and remember that every step forward brings you closer to the financial freedom you desire.

If you find this book helpful, please leave a favorable review for the book on Amazon.

Thank you, and Good Luck.

www.ingramcontent.com/pod-product-compliance
Lightning Source LLC
Chambersburg PA
CBHW071005290526
45795CB00005B/1780